Spirit Balm

An uplifting collection of
he**Art** and soul **Poetry**

By Stephanie Toler

"Unalome Lotus"

Artwork from this book may be purchased at: www.StephanieToler.com

ISBN: 978-0-578-29193-2

Anandamaya Press

Dedication

May these poems bring more love, compassion, and beauty into this world.

Lucy, I pray these words serve to comfort and inspire you as you move through life's incredible journey. Know that you are perfect as you are and you are loved beyond measure.

Acknowledgments

To my beloved Patrick. I am grateful for the grounding, love, inspiration, wisdom, and support that you provide always, in all ways. What a blessing to share this journey with you.

To my dear Omi who initiated my spiritual path.

Thank you to Kathryn Brethauer, Elizabeth Skovran, Peter Colclasure, Jessica Bentley, Ryan McNeace, and all of my dear friends and family for your love and support.

May this book serve the highest good.

Table of Contents

Dedication...iv

Acknowledgments..iv

Table of Contents...v

Part 1: Release 2

    Unreality..3

    Unholy Ghost 4

    Mom's Poem 6

    The Wait 8

    Healing Moon 10

    Surrender 12

    Presence 14

    Parting 15

    Where Can It Be? 16

Part II: Awakening...18

    Everything I Know 19

    The Wheel 20

    Yes, But You Will Love More 21

    Seeds 23

    Sensing Divine...26

    Open...31

    Choices...33

    Oops! Did I Offend Someone? 34

    Wake Up! Wake Up! 36

    What's Real?...38

Shining...39

Who You Really Are 41

Old Stories...44

New Moon Alchemy Prayer...........................46

Life Was Always Precious 48

Part III: Beloved Other 50

A Love Poem...51

Talk To Me..53

My Man of Stars..55

Into The Flow..57

Manna..60

You're Beautiful..61

Expressions 62

Blessings..63

Part IV: Natural Order 64

Intentions 65

My Hands...67

Where To?..68

In Gratitude 70

Endless...71

Elemental Love 73

When I Die 74

Part 1: Release

"The Lightworkers"

Unreality

Low belly growls
Sifting through meat
Nightfall fruit drops
All sugar
No Heat

Golden veil rises
Shimmering shining
Rips in the
Lining
Silvery Slips

Where has it gone now?
Tricky track tracking
Moody blues
Stacking
White Noise

Caressing lines blindly
Holding on tightly
Chugging time
Timely
All Aboard

Girly girl twirling
Everything swirling
Speckled spark
Sparkling
It's gone

Shhhhhhh
There is nothing to hold onto.

Unholy Ghost

Unholy Ghost,
Why do you hide
In the once-fertile garden
Of my collapsing heart?

Unwelcome guest,
Serpent disguised.
Are you waiting to steal
The tears from my eyes?

This land was made
For beauty to be grown
But you're taking the life
From the seeds I have sown.

What can I give
To place you at rest?
To keep you from taking
The light from my chest?

Unholy Ghost,
Are we karmically bound?
How can I wash your
Scent from my ground?

I know who you are and
I've asked you to leave.
Has my heart not had
Enough of your grief?

"Heart On Her Sleeve" (Self-portrait)

Mom's Poem

A tear rolls down our face
Not of sadness, but of grace
I say ours, for mine is yours
Memories flow within each trace

We fought, we cried, we acted out
Your fire scorched my childish pout
We struggled our entire life
Caught in pain, tangled in doubt

I wouldn't accept that you had tried
Until long after you had died
Your death removed a heavy veil
Compassion replaced my useless pride

I feel you more than I knew I could
I love you more than I thought I should
Our tender heart relieved by peace
Your soul alive in motherhood

You whispered softly as I slept
You held me warmly as I wept
You carry on within my soul
Maternal love now resurrect

"B(Earth)"

Three months after my mother passed away, in 2016, I had a vision: I saw both of us, corpses underground connected by an umbilical cord through which love, light, and compassion were flowing. Above ground was a huge pile of garbage, but it wasn't touching us.

*I immediately realized the garbage was all of our issues, our shared drama, and that even *all of that* couldn't touch our cosmic connection, represented by the umbilical cord. Our bodies underground represented the temporal nature of this earthly incarnation.*

The Wait

My dear God, why torture me so?
Your smile reveals, then away it flows
And despite all my searching, I know not where it goes.

I wait for your call, I wait all alone
I wait in the dark, still as a stone
And though I sit by your fire, I'm chilled to the bone.

I feel your presence, I know you are here
Yet despite the silence, you hide from my ear
While I long to be free, I'm trapped in fear.

Have I not surrendered myself at your feet?
Have I not offered my very heart beat?
What more can I do to be warmed by your heat?

I have tried so hard to show you my love
I have worked so hard to rise above
But my wings are clipped, I'm a grounded dove.

Please take it all, take all that I have
It weighs me down as I move on this path
While I journey towards your healing salve.

I am short on ideas, nothing left to do
Perhaps this is where I'll finally find truth
I lay myself down.

I wait for You.

"Ganesha, Remover of Obstacles"

Healing Moon

The moon so bright
      it looked like dawn
As the night carried
      on and on

I couldn't sleep so
      I gazed awhile
La Luna melting
      me to a smile

Soft white clouds
      gone rolling by
Like angels watching
      from the sky

My thankful prayer
      I shared aloud
Dear God…
Please root me in
      the here and now

From here I must
      release regret
Release the bonds
      of this karmic debt

Heal my body
      Heal my heart
May all that haunts me
      break apart

Let your light
      shine brightly through
So that I may now
      walk with you

"Moon Garden I: Healing Moon"

Surrender

All I've ever known is slipping from my grasp
Beneath it is a whisper…
"Let go of that which is going."

My hands and mind have been like magic wands
Creating all I've ever wanted
But the magic never lasts.

Ego creations glimmer fancy in the moonlight
When no shadow is cast
Then quickly decay in the sun…

And, so. I try something new: I give it all up to God.
Naked and scared; I ask:
"Where then, am I going?"

There is a whisper above it all, *"Surrender…*
There is nowhere to go.
All is coming, Love."

"Awakened Heart"

Presence

From my hands flow everything
The eternal unfolding of my heart
In joy, all arises and in sorrow, falls away
There is nothing old, nothing new
In perfect stillness, I remain

Parting

It's been a while since we've spoken
You're going your way
And I'm going mine
It seems our world has broken
And it's tearing at the threads of time

Life was never predictable
But we've never seen anything
Like this before
And rather than hold onto the shore
I'm releasing into the flow

I know not when we'll meet again
But I know you've been
A longtime friend
And though our paths are parting
I'll love you until the end

Where Can It Be?

Looking, looking
Where can it be?
She's looked so much
She can no longer see

Seeking, seeking
All the time taking
She's pushed herself
To the point of breaking

Clinging, clinging
Always needs more
She needs so much
Nothing sticks to her core

Hoping, hoping
Her mind is still coping
And what is it that
Her spirit is holding?

Praying, praying
Can anyone hear?
Begging so loudly
She's drowning in fear

Breaking, breaking
Held on for too long
There's no room here
For will other than God's

(Cont.)

Where Can It Be? (Cont.)

Folding, folding
There's nothing to do
She must rest and wait
For her spirit renewed

Giving, giving
She gave it all up
The past now emptied
There's room in her cup

Breathing, breathing
Take it all in
Filling with love
She's filling within

Part II: Awakening

"The Great Awakening"

Everything I Know

I promise,
What you seek is not out there.

It's here.
It's home.

Look inside and you will find
Your throne.

The Wheel

The tiniest speck spins out to the edge
And finds itself back at center again

Only to move even deeper inside
The breadth of spirit narrowing wide

We seek without what we have within
Still knowing the places we have not been

It often feels like a harrowing ride
Until our misperceptions have died

Once we know to stop turning the wheel
Finally then does the truth reveal

Yes, But You Will Love More

Yes,
> The pain digs down deep.

But,
> If you are patient and allow it,

You Will
> Feel its new-carved reservoirs fill with

Love…
> Only next time, there will be

More.

"Wisdom Balances An Open Heart"

Seeds

It was I who started the fire.
I admit, I was careless when
I decided to plant those seeds.

Yes, I could have been more thoughtful.

I wasn't paying attention.
I didn't realize they would
Strangle out the warm sun.

Yes, I could have planned better.

So I burned my garden down.
It wasn't easy to do and in fact,
It was hard to see it all go.

Yes, I should have known better by now.

What a blaze that roared!
So big and out of control,
Burning up everything around.

Yes, I could have been more careful.

The sky was hazy with ash.
I couldn't see or hear a thing.
Neither could anyone else.

Yes, I was sad and ashamed.

(Cont.)

Seeds (Cont.)

But the skies are clearing!
I can see the shining sun and now
I can hear the birds singing.

Yes, I'll find my way again.

Oh, the lessons learned!
The soil is fertile once more.
And I will be a better gardener.

"Death Brings New Life"

Sensing Divine

Mother India,
>how tragic you are
To those who can't see
>straight into your heart.

I had heard of the filth,
>tales of garbage abound;
Calves casually scattering
>brown mounds on the ground.

Your smells, they could turn
>brave men running for home,
but what a shame it would be
>to know your stench all alone.

Your horns, they exhaust
>our sensitive ears.
And for a lonesome traveler,
>may be all that he hears.

What a shame it would be
>for one not to trace,
all that belies
>your mistreated face.

But what a feast you are
>to my senses and heart.
Though I must admit,
>they rebelled at the start.

(Cont.)

Sensing Divine (Cont.)

As I dance through your alleys
  how sad it would be,
for this to be all
  my eyes, they would see.

When around every corner,
  new landscapes await!
Here lies a calf
  amongst golden gates.

A temple, a palace, an arch,
  Now a shrine!
Your streets, they call out
  your spirit, divine!

A sitar, a tabla…
  exotic, their tones
Notes sharply reaching
  deep into my bones.

A dog, she sets off
  a galloping horse.
The children unfazed
  by this chaotic force.

Your kin, did you say…
  His body "expired"?
I wonder, did he get
  his freedom desired?

(Cont.)

Sensing Divine (Cont.)

Swiftly we move…
  Lord, I hope we don't crash!
This seems like a place
  where pedestrians pass!

The smoke calmly billows,
  but what does he make?
Pakoras and naan!!!
  I would love such a taste!

Hanuman sits on his
  banyan branch throne.
Looking to take
  my meal for his own.

Drawn into a shop
  by delights for my nose
An incense bouquet,
  nag champa and rose!

Your women, so lovely,
  so cheerfully dressed!
They smile as though
  I'm their personal guest.

Donning silver and gold,
  emerald, chartreuse
How I delight
  in their various hues.

(Cont.)

Sensing Divine (Cont.)

So much I have seen
       but I sense there is more.
More treasures are waiting
       for me to explore.

You've shared of your heart
       and I offer you mine.
With a prayer these memories
       stay vibrant in time.

"Goddess Lakshmi"

Open

When we close our minds to that now unknown
We close ourselves to perspective grown

It's convenient to think that we know what's best
But we limit ourselves, evolution arrest

Isn't it worth having choices, more?
As we open ourselves to a life explored?

When our minds are free, come spirit's bright gifts
Which hold the secret to our own true bliss

"Samadhi"

Choices

I hear the judgment in his voice
But quickly see I have a choice

To let his words be part of me
Or leave them there to simply be

The thoughts he shares are his alone
And come from somewhere I've outgrown

So why be pulled into the deep
When love alone is mine to keep

Oops! Did I Offend Someone?

No, I don't care about
        my reputation,
Biased observations
        that go round and round.

Fragile birdie flew away
        because I had to say
The—*my*—truth.
        Is that all it takes?

My Scorpio nature
        won't coddle a stranger
I won't coddle family either.
        It's just not who I am.

I won't take your shit.
        You need to handle it.
Take responsibility.
        I will do the same.

Don't like it?
        Then don't come around me.
I deal in authenticity.
        Fulllll Stop.

And No,
        I'm not afraid
Of the things you might say
        To the community.

(Cont.)

Oops! Did I Offend Someone? (Cont.)

I know who I am.
        I know where I stand.
And I will not dance around
        Your sensitivity.

For what it's worth
        I will express my truth.
So take a good look at you
        And I will keep looking at me.

Wake Up! Wake Up!

Wake up! Wake up!
It's time to break up
With all the dark energy
Filling our cups

We live in such stress
It turns to distress
Then turns to disease
Our bodies a mess

There is a known cure
We've heard it before
Turn off "The News"
And open the door

Step on outside
The dark will subside
Once the sun's light
Can open our eyes

Look out! Look out!
It's all coming now
We can let it release
We can give it a shout!

Nature won't mind
Her patience divine
She takes it from us
And transmutes it in time

(Cont.)

Wake Up! Wake Up! (Cont.)

There is a new way
With each dawning day
To fill up our lives
With beauty and play

Breathe in the fresh air
Be the love that we share
Connect more with Earth
All the better we'll fare

What's Real?

I'm beyond tired
>of BOTH sides
Left or Right,
>so polarized

The truth remains
>we come, we go
It's all part of
>the Maya show

Everyone caught
>in a grand illusion
Can't separate truth
>from their own delusion

Turn off the telly
>to hear what's real
The sound of silence
>can truly heal

Make peace within
>and forget the rest
Or stay outward-engaged
>and you'll fail the test

Your body's a vessel
>Your mind is a trick
Your spirit, the mystery
>Is making you tick

Shining

I came close despite my fear
To touch the hand I knew was near.
Bathing me in eternal light
So I might stand here shining bright.

But first I understood the dark
Could not deceive this divine spark.
And so I walked into the fire
Tending to my heart's desire.

"Passionate Heart"

Who You Really Are

The past is gone
Don't try to hold on
I've been calling you back home

Back to your roots
Where you'll find the truth
Of who you really are

You are no woman of the world
Easily lost
With no light to guide your way

You know where you've been
Now see where you're going
Born Anew. Born Anew.

You are Sister of the Earth
Lady of the Land
In touch with Nature's Way

Tell me…
How do the violet and clover taste?
Are the berries sweet?

Wash your sorrows in the river, Dear One
And tell me…
Does the rock feel smooth underfoot?

(Cont.)

Who You Really Are (Cont.)

Return back to your home.
Paint the birds. Paint the trees.
Pay homage with your life.

The past is gone
Don't try to hold on
I've been calling you back home

Back to your roots
Where you'll find the truth
Of who you really are

"Pachamama"

Old Stories

Old stories swirling
       through the air
I don't mean to be rude but
       I really don't care.

Even my own,
       they bore me to tears,
Or worse ~ they remind me of
       my old, programmed fears.

The past has gone now.
       Let's leave it alone.
We can never go back.
       We can only come home.

If we really must speak,
       let's create something new:
A world full of peace, love,
       forgiveness, and truth.

"Sshhh"

New Moon Alchemy Prayer

On this new moon I pray to you
    for paradigm alchemy
From swirling dust to cosmic love ~
    please help my eyes to see

We've come so far from Heaven's stars,
    this dream that dreams with open eyes
Unconscious play goes on and on
    The world's adrift and so am I

Wake us from this senseless state
    to know our power within
To make the change you wish of us
    and Heaven to Earth we'll bring

Let separation melt away
    and the joy of life emerge
With all our senses knowing truth
    we'll rise above our hurts

The past will fade; the now so pure
    when Spirit reigns supreme
This is what I pray for us:
    that Love will set us free.

"Queen of Hearts"

Life Was Always Precious

Cancer.
It's hardly the answer
I was looking for

Yet it seems to
have opened
a door

To my deepest Self
Filled with the infinite wealth
of Divinity

So, if you see me
Please don't tell me
to "Fight"

Let's keep it Light
So I can LOVE myself
Back to health

Life was ALWAYS
Fragile
ALWAYS Precious

And I have every
Intention
To live it

With Beauty
With Grace
And with Gratitude

"Green Tara"

I began this painting on the day I received my diagnosis, as a prayer for health and a mental health practice to cope with my distress. By the end of this 21-day painting meditation, the tumor had been surgically removed, and I was on a healing path.

Part III: Beloved Other

"Mermaids"

Painted for my daughter, Lucy.

A Love Poem

You never asked for a poem. How would you know?
That when my love runs deep, the poetry flows.
From the top of these hills so vibrantly green
It tumbles down low to the powerful sea...
And all of the Earth our feet have yet to tread
Every little bit is covered in my love.

And so...
It is not a poem I should give you, but a map
A map of my love that starts with me and ends with you.

Or... does it start with you and end with me?
We're so enmeshed, it's hard to see!
But it has no start and it has no end.
It moves through us, around us, and back once again.
My love, our love encircles the Earth and
My love, our love knows no bounds.

And so...
There simply is no map that I can share
But you have my heart, wide open and bare.

"Winged Heart"

Talk To Me

Whisper your sweet nothings
Held tender to my ear
Seduce me with your passion
It's all I want to hear

I've always been a sucker
For a slow poetic pace
Let me feast upon your thoughts
Let me lie in their embrace

Your words make their way
A fervent beating in my chest
There's nothing more romantic
Than love that's been expressed

"Gustavo's Roses"

My Man of Stars

Written for my beloved on Valentine's Day 2019 from Santa Marta, Colombia -
"The Heart of the World."

Come,
My Man of Stars
Heart of Sun
Son of Heart
Come cover me
with your Wildness!

Let's roll around
Tangled
Hips and Lips
Hearts and Parts
Let us make thunder
and shake the skies!

Wrapped in
Ephemeral bliss
Let our luscious love
Overflow
From the Heart
of the World.

"Beloved Patrick"

Inspired by his big, beautiful heart.

"Behold thine immortal Self resurrected with Christ in the light of illumination,
present in every soul, every flower, every atom!"
~ Paramhansa Yogananda

Into The Flow

Written for Lucy

Yes,
I'll take you with me
Into the flow,
      Sweet Baby.

I need to move!
I need to stretch!
The music grooves.
      Vinyasa!

But then a small cry
So I don't even try.
We both know
      This is really your flow.

You don't want stillness.
And so yoga becomes
A booty-shaking
      Dance party!

I can dance all night.
And we do for a while,
But when you slow down
      Momma knows.

You want to lay down
And nurse the hour away.
Both of us lulled into
      This milky flow.

(Cont.)

Into The Flow (Cont.)

I bring you to my chest,
Latched to my breast
Where we slip into
     A most DIVINE rest.

I'll never mind
Giving you my time.
Just grateful to know
     That together we flow.

"My Beloved Child"

Manna

Dearest one,
My love to hold
Made for you
This milky gold

Manna flowing
From my breast
This loving heart
Beats through my chest

We make the space
Connection strong
You'll have the ground
A life's built on

Healing our
Ancestral line
Breaking from
The bonds of time

Healing hearts
Our true intent
To turn around
All past neglect

We heal ourselves
We heal the world
While I nurse
My baby girl

You're Beautiful.

Hey, you, yes, you! Who's to say?
That you should look a certain way
From my eyes over here
You look perfectly okay.

And in fact…

You're beautiful in every way!

Expressions

Often a bold passion's felt
The desire to express oneself
May you always share this wealth
With an open heart and mind

Some will disapprove of you
There's nothing for this that you can do
That's for them to self-pursue
While you make art from life

No one else can shut you down
It's up to you to stand your ground
Remember you're not lost, but found
Within the wellspring of your soul

I pray that you stay always true
To the spirit dwelling inside of you
Of all the hurts, there's nothing new
On the surface of this earth

Let the years roll on, my love
Life is nothing to tire of
Keep your eyes fixed up above
The clamor of this world

Something unique within your soul
Yearns for you to release control
In the end, there is no goal
But a life that's well-expressed.

Blessings

Dear Mother-Father-God, Great Spirit:

Thank you. We are eternally grateful for this life that you've bestowed upon us.

We pray that all lives be blessed with health, joy, peace, love, harmony, creativity, intimacy, beauty, alignment with nature and with our own true spirits.

May our eyes, hearts, and minds continually take in the beauty around us as we bless this world with your grace.

May we sing freely, create authentically, and live with a sense of deep purpose and fulfillment, while knowing all that is good and true in the world.

May we feel secure in your presence and in ourselves as we walk freely and confidently along our paths.

May we always know that we are perfect and loved, exactly as we are.

May we all heal and grow in love and togetherness for the rest of our days.

Blessings on our lives.

Aho, may it be so.

Part IV: Natural Order

"Renewal" (Self-portrait)

Intentions

Overtaken
by a wave of change
The moon ever-tugging
on my heart

Swept up into
the flow of life
The past-now-forever
pulled apart

Sunlight has come
beaming in
Sweetness bubbles
through my lips

Life as I have
never known
now created
at my fingertips

"Moon Garden 2: Intentions"

My Hands

These galactivated hands
I know to be Divine
Are bringing forth the patterns
I see with my mind's eye.

Active blue energy swirls
Like magnets in my hands
Shine the vibrant light of truth
When even I don't understand.

They push-pull with the moon
They whisper "Cho Ku Rei"
They create Divine transmissions
Working as they pray.

These hands were always meant
To create, to love, to heal
They were made to celebrate
The mystery revealed.

Where To?

I used to feel like I was running *from* something.
Now I feel like I'm running *to* something.

This something is a mystery.
But it better be ready.

Because, when I get there,
I'm smothering it in kisses.

It's taking me on the most beautiful journey.

"Path of the Heart"

In Gratitude

Awake alone in this early hour
The birds, they sing for me

The dewy air fills my lungs
And I am nourished by its Qi

Wind-blown leaves spiral down
A prompting for the day

To release all that's come before
And for this, my heart does pray

Love surrounds to hold me close
My soul sings to the sky

More grateful for this life I live
With each day that passes by

Endless

The core of Earth runs through my veins
Its rivers through my womb
And when this fire burns away
Dear Earth becomes my tomb

The air I breathe dissolves my mind
The winds of change refresh
And once the leaves all blow away
The past leaves through my breath

The moon, she glows within my heart
Our rhythm in perfect phase
Cycling through the ebb and flow
Of life's unending ways

For all my wants, the land provides
Nourishing and sweet
Its seasons carry me back home
Full circle and complete

"Spring Nettles"

Elemental Love

I demanded of the heavens above,
"Tell me, how do I live in your love
When something still exists in me,
That wants to build walls in between?"

The answer came, pure and true:
"Look around for what to do."

And so I asked the tumbling stream,
"How can I let this love be seen?"
"Go with the flow, but look around,
You can still be solid, like the ground."

I looked to the earth and heard her say,
"I give my fruits freely, day after day."

To the trees I said, "Your roots are shared."
"Not only that, but we clear the air."
Creatures abound, wild and free
Whispered for me to simply be me.

I still wasn't sure that this was enough,
To which they replied, "You're already Love."

When I Die

I pray that when I die
I am ready to go
That no part of me whispers
No... no... no...

When death knocks at my door
I will feel into my core
Knowing there is more
As I let my spirit pour out

Love all over my family
Love all over my friends
Let my love flood the world
That this love may never end

That my body shed its pain
My mind, no longer vain
That I am free to soar
And my love will still remain

No clinging to the earth
No purpose left unfurled
But an earnest life well-lived
Given all I had to give

Love all over my family
Love all over my friends
Let my love flood the world
That this love may never end

"Full Circle"